WITH JE

I am Calm

This book belongs to:

....

....

Copyrights

WITH JESUS
I am Calm
Coloring Book Edition

Good News Meditations Kids

To receive print-ready samples from the coloring book
version of this book, please go to gnmkids.com/free

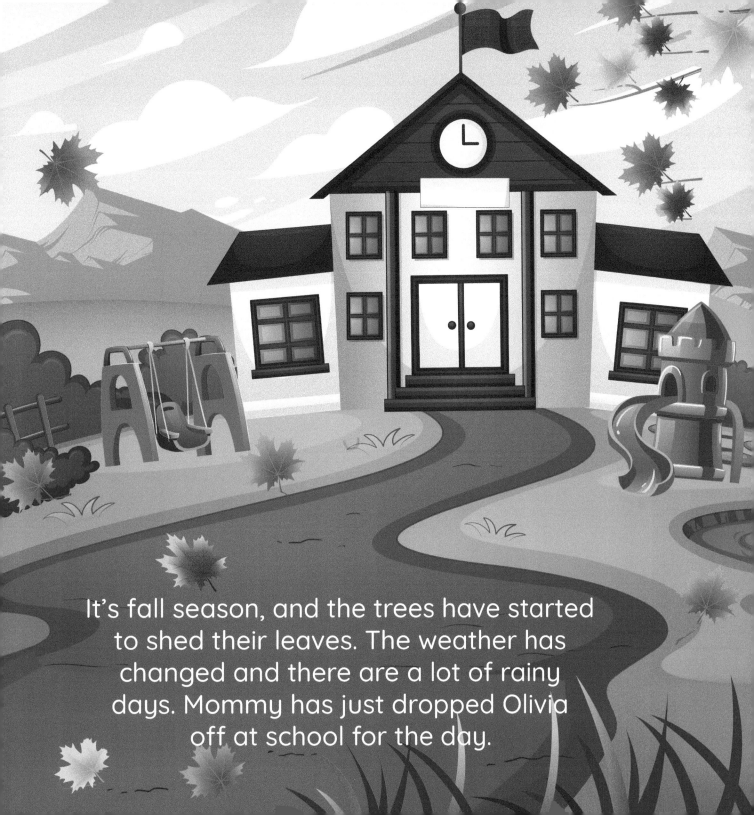

It's fall season, and the trees have started to shed their leaves. The weather has changed and there are a lot of rainy days. Mommy has just dropped Olivia off at school for the day.

Olivia can't wait to go outside and play in the backyard. She is eager to go down the slides and play with her friends.

"Oh no!" Olivia's teacher exclaims. She tells the kids that they won't be able to go outside because it is raining. Olivia is disappointed. She gets angry and starts yelling, "It's not fair! I want to go out and play!"

Her teacher tries to calm her down and invites her to join the other kids so they can read a book together, but Olivia is not happy with that. She is so angry and upset that she sits in a corner with a frown on her face.

Later that day, Olivia tells her mommy what happened. When she is done talking, Mommy tells her a story.

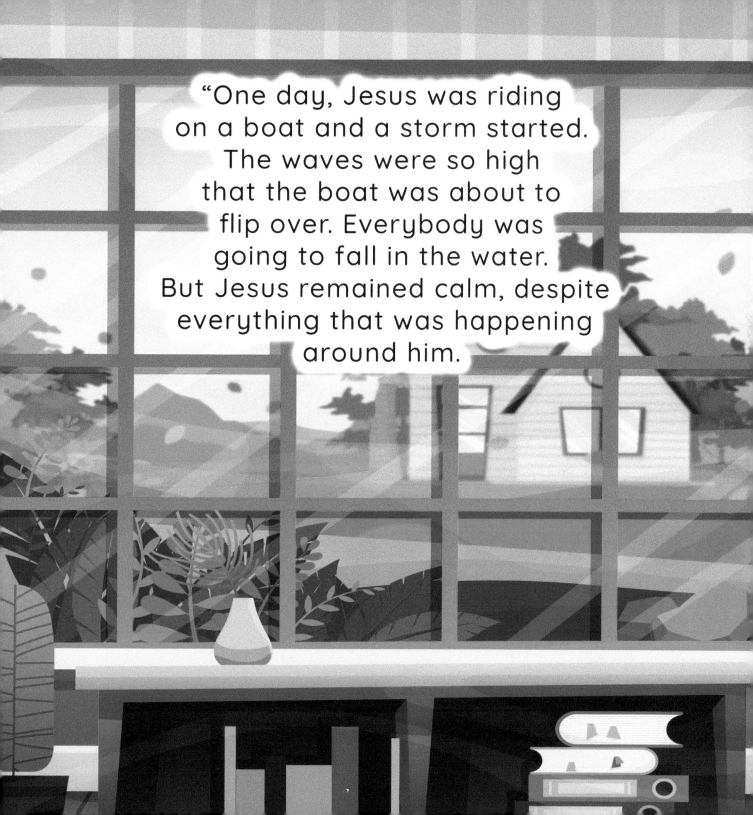

"One day, Jesus was riding on a boat and a storm started. The waves were so high that the boat was about to flip over. Everybody was going to fall in the water. But Jesus remained calm, despite everything that was happening around him.

"Wow, Mommy, Jesus was a superhero!" Olivia exclaims. "I believe Jesus can help me to be just like Him and remain calm the next time something upsetting happens to me."

Mommy smiles. "Yes, exactly! You have the same peace Jesus had to remain calm when you are upset about something."

The next day, just as all the kids
are about to go out, it starts raining again.
This time, Olivia remembers the story
of Jesus on the boat and how calm he'd
remained. Olivia takes a deep breath
and tells herself, "With Jesus... I am calm."

She remains calm enough to take part in all the activities of the day. Olivia is so proud of herself. She realizes that she can remain calm at any time, especially when things don't always go her way.
The End.

And he arose, and rebuked the wind,
and said unto the sea, Peace, be still.
And the wind ceased, and there was
a great calm.

Mark 4v39 KJV

Author's note:

Thank you so much for reading this book. If you enjoyed this book, we would love it if you could leave a review and recommend it to a friend.

If there is anything you would like to share with us to help us improve this book, please go to gnmkids.com/feedback

WITH JESUS

I am Calm
Coloring Book Edition

Good News Meditations Kids

To receive print-ready samples from the coloring book version of this book, please go to gnmkids.com/free

Please checkout our other books

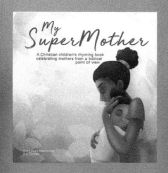

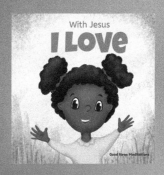

www.gnmkids.com